Jean Spencer

A Retrospective Exhibition

The Yarrow Gallery
Oundle School

September 2006

This catalogue is published to accompany the exhibition

Jean Spencer
A Retrospective Exhibition

From 22 September to 14 October 2006
The Yarrow Gallery, Oundle School, Northamptonshire.

Curated by John McGowan

Catalogue designed and edited by John McGowan and David Fuller

Photographs by John McGowan and from the estate of Jean Spencer, by kind permission of Mrs M. Waters

The Yarrow Gallery
Oundle School
Oundle
PE8 4GH
Tel: 01832 277170
Fax: 01832 277170
www.oundleschool.org.uk

ISBN 0-9518925-1-7
         978-0-9518925-1-0
Published by Oundle School

Printed by Stanley L. Hunt (Printers) Limited, Rushden, Northamptonshire. Edition of 2000

Contents

Curator's Notes

Jean Spencer was one of my art lecturers at Bulmershe College, Reading, in the late 1960s. This exhibition is a tribute to a fine artist and an inspiring teacher.

This brochure is intended as an accompaniment to the exhibition rather than just a catalogue of its contents. There are works shown in it which have not been exhibited previously and have been included to give a wider notion of Jean Spencer's achievement.

My personal thanks go to Oundle School for giving me the opportunity to organise this exhibition and publish this brochure, which we hope will have a wide circulation and re-confirm Jean Spencer's place in the continuing constructivist project.

Acknowledgements

Oundle School is grateful for the help and encouragement given to this project by Mrs Marian Waters, Jean Spencer's sister. She has given up much of her time to assist with this exhibition project and, in the recent past, to look after the bequest of her work. Thanks are also due to the other members of the family, who have lent so generously to this exhibition.

Michael Harrison is the Director of Kettle's Yard Gallery, Cambridge, and worked with Jean Spencer on the "Testing the System" exhibition in 1996 – the last to feature her work in Britain in her lifetime. Michael wrote the obituary in *The Independent* newspaper, which is here expanded to give greater context to her work.

Elizabeth Chaplin is a sociologist and writes from her experience of working with Jean Spencer in the "Countervail" group. She gives a personal perspective on her as an artist and co-worker.

Dr Alan Fowler is an art historian and contributed to the catalogue for "Elements of Abstraction", a recent survey of British Abstract Art at Southampton City Art Gallery. Here he puts the "Systems" group into historical perspective.

Sir Nicholas Serota is Director of Tate and curated the "Systems" exhibition in 1972 at the Whitechapel Gallery. He was responsible for the selection and exhibition of Jean Spencer's work at Tate Britain in 1999.

Double Square Painting Nos 1 and 2 have been loaned with the kind permission of the Master and Fellows of Churchill College, Cambridge University. *Four Part Painting No 1* has been kindly loaned by Dr Andrew Webber of Churchill College. We are also grateful for the loans from the Reading Museum Service, Reading Borough Council, The Slade School of Art and private collections.

John McGowan
Oundle School

Jean Spencer/Malcom Hughes, Tate Britain installation 1999 Photo © Tate 1999

Foreword

Jean Spencer's paintings lie on the boundary between reason and emotion, logic and intuition, and order and expression. In art such polarities are sometimes less distant from each other than is often assumed. The hot insistent colour of Donald Judd's late work cannot be explained by reference solely to the conventions and tenets of minimalism any more than we can adequately ascribe the magisterial achievement of Cy Twombly's successive cycles of paintings over a long career solely to the workings of an unfettered "abstract expressionist" hand. All art is the product of a subtly shifting balance between the rational and the irrational, between what we "know" and what we "feel".

Jean Spencer began her career as an artist who used the rules of number and mathematics to explore rhythm and sequence, accentuated by the fall of light and shadow on the pure white or neutral surfaces of her reliefs. Extended exercises in pencil on paper prepared the way, followed by a careful choice of a precise white or of materials such as aluminium which are self-coloured and reflect the light without further intervention by the artist. These early works explore the possibilities of building a composition with a limited range of elements, a process akin to developing a simple melody and then exploring its potential through repetition, elaboration and layering of the notes. Her methodology was close in spirit to the work of those "minimalist" composers of the early seventies, such as Steve Reich, whom Jean so admired.

However, in the late seventies colour came to assume an increasingly important and then dominant place in her investigation into the properties of the physical world. Her regard for the colour investigations of earlier and more senior artists working in the tradition of constructivism, including Malevich and the Swiss artist Richard Paul Lohse, did not inhibit the development of her own distinctive palette. Like Malcolm Hughes, her partner in art and life for nearly forty years, Jean was also fascinated by the way in which the old masters, and especially Nicolas Poussin, deployed colour. Gradually she became absorbed by the properties of colour and pigment, and by the cognitive systems through which the eye translates the phenomenon of colour to the brain and thence, through our cultural experience, to a reading of the world.

Jean's deep engagement in her own work was complemented by an interest in the work of others. She was one of the original members of the "Systems" group and from the late seventies her strengths as a teacher and organiser came to the fore. She played an increasingly influential role in the activities of those associations of artists working in the constructivist tradition. In England she was a co-founder of "Countervail" and in Europe she promoted exchange with artists in what was then Eastern Europe, long before the "new internationalism" became fashionable in the nineties.

Her own increasing interest in colour encouraged deep reflection on the theory, rules and properties of colour, but she also recognised that there were attributes of colour that could not be so ordered, premeditated or regulated. In 1996 she spoke of colour as having "both a logic and a jouissance", or joy, "both its own law and the power to subvert the law that artists and scientists place upon it."

In her final works Spencer achieved an extraordinary presence, intensity and freshness of colour. However, the strengths of these works reveal themselves only slowly. As Spencer herself wrote, "These paintings formalise the time of looking ... All paintings unfold in time, they are not so different to music or poetry or film, or the space/time continuum of a building ...". At first sight Jean Spencer's paintings may appear deceptively simple, but with attention and patience come depth and infinite reward.

Nicholas Serota

1970: Systems, gouache

Jean Mary Spencer, Artist and Educator

For many artists in the sixties and seventies teaching was the lifeline which financed studio practice, but for Jean Spencer a commitment to both was there from the outset. At Bath Academy of Art (1960-63), at that time in Corsham, she took a teacher training course in art instead of straight fine art. She then went on to teach at Bulmershe College of Higher Education in Reading (1968-88), before a ten-year stint at the Slade School of Fine Art as Tutor to Students and Secretary to the School, and from 1995 also as Reader in Fine Art.

In the Sixth Form she had decided that Art was for her, and her other A level subjects, Maths and English Literature, remained of almost equal importance throughout her life. Her artistic path was decided in her second year at Bath when Malcolm Hughes and John Ernest, as tutors, introduced her to the world of systematic constructivism with which she engaged immediately. The labels of that kind of art would change, as would her work, over the next thirty-five years, but for the rest of her life hers was to be an abstract constructive art, founded in rationality and in strong egalitarian conviction.

The early works were white reliefs, often articulated by numerical sequences, but in the mid-1970s she became interested in colour because, as she said, "There comes a point when the sorts of things that you want to say about how something relates to something else ... become extremely complex." She took on colour, not as a means of coding, but in all its unfathomable fullness. Painting was a matter of dealing with a question or a problem whose answer would be found in pictorial resolution. In an interview she talked about a four-part set of paintings made in 1992: "I wanted to deal with deep violet as a problem and make a painting which starts with that deep violet." Those paintings were of equal, "egalitarian" bands, but more recently she played, against all constructivist orthodoxy, with our tendency to seek an object and a ground, and with the interchange between the two. "I wanted certain boundaries to be seen as though under dispute; I wanted colour alignments to countervail geometric divisions; I wanted an asymmetry of composition to offer, perhaps, some resolution to the asymmetries inherent in the colour array; and all this 'legally', that is within a system against which individual judgements can be made." The cerebral and the emotional were as important as each other and she was acutely aware that, while her paintings involved the detachment of rules or systems, they drew life from the contingencies of fleeting light and the active collaboration of the people looking at them. "You only get interest out if you invest!" she remarked.

Collaboration and exchange were always important. Spencer was the youngest member of the Systems Group whose activities reached their climax in an Arts Council touring exhibition, first shown at the Whitechapel Gallery in 1972. In the 1970s and 1980s she participated in Arbeitskreis, an international workshop for systematic constructive art, founded by Ewerdt Hilgemann and with Richard Paul Lohse as a guiding light. The exhibitions, symposia and practical workshops brought together artists from separate traditions of constructivism, and left her a committed European and internationalist. Indeed, she exhibited more frequently elsewhere in Europe than in England. What she saw as "an ideal kind of collaboration" came about from 1983 when Ray Thomson's Whitechapel studio would be converted each month into Exhibiting Space where artists, architects, theoreticians, historians, linguists, musicians *et al.* would gather in an attempt to break down the barriers between art practice and art theory, and to explore connections with other disciplines. Like all such groups, Exhibiting Space came to an end, this one in conflict between those who wanted things defined and those, including Spencer, who sought a constant process of redefinition.

Spencer's egalitarian commitment led naturally to feminism and to ardent support for other women artists. It was she who came up with the title "Countervail", adopted from Julia Kristeva's "Giotto's Joy", for a grouping of women artists which had sprung out of interviews with the sociologist Elizabeth Chaplin. They took issue with the mainstream feminist position, that all forms of rationality were antipathetic to women. As Spencer confessed, "I don't think at any point we came to a comfortable solution to that", but discussions led on to Jean initiating a "Postal Academy", and to a successful series of exhibitions and seminars in Sheffield, and at Warwick and York Universities.

Spencer was the epitome of the artist-researcher, always curious and enquiring, and invariably bubbling with the excitement of some new connection found. In 1978-79 she took time out to do an MA in the History and Theory of Art at Sussex University and is remembered as a student of daunting intelligence and depth. She read and re-read Proust, loved Bach, and found interest in early narrative opera, particularly Handel. And that engagement with narrative and with time in its apprehension formed a major part of a study of Giotto's Arena Chapel which was far advanced but incomplete when she died. All this fed into her painting.

It is some achievement to have got this far having mentioned Malcolm Hughes only once. The tutor became partner and eventually husband, and theirs was one of those remarkable artistic partnerships which allowed each their independence, and whose kitchen in Putney was second home for many an artist and musician. They shared a passion for bicycles and for his seventieth birthday Jean offered Malcolm a trip to a place of his choice to see the Tour de France. A few years later they were to cycle the breadth of England, admittedly at its narrowest, but probably its hilliest point, ending up at Durham Cathedral.

Jean's death in January 1998 was a tragic sequel to that of Malcolm, also from cancer, in September 1997. Over the previous five years and more they had been the driving force and vision behind a project which led to the exhibition "Testing the System" at Kettle's Yard in Cambridge, followed by a symposium, "Patterns of Connection", and an exhibition of the paintings of Richard Paul Lohse. Their last summer was spent with Jean, for once free of educational duties, as Kettle's Yard Artist Fellow at Churchill College, and Malcolm in attendance. The last blue of the six paintings which Jean made in Cambridge was applied under her instruction by Trevor Clark in the week before she died.

A Postscript

Reading this obituary eight years on I'm reminded how much Jean Spencer did not fit the standard image of the constructive or systematic artist. In her time at Cambridge, in the last summer of her life, she gave a lunchtime talk about Kettle's Yard and its creator, Jim Ede. With its bare wooden floors and white walls, Kettle's Yard is sometimes taken to be a product of English puritanism, but Jean saw, beyond its sparseness, a rich expression of delight in the things of life as spiritual experience. She identified something of the Franciscan in Ede and, I suspect, also in herself. Perhaps there remained a modicum of the Methodist upbringing in Ede's notoriously simple hospitality, but there was nothing ascetic in the simplicity of Jean and Malcolm's entertainment, expressed in good whisky and the finest shortbread.

Jean, like Ede, was a social being, enjoying discussion and sometimes quite heated debate among colleagues. But she craved time in her own company, working quietly in her studio. There the dialogue was with her painting, and the painting itself was a matter of dialogue, with ideas and rules coming to terms with the physical reality of pigment, linen and stretchers. Colour in constructive or systematic painting has tended towards a differentiation of elements; even Kenneth Martin's wonderful late paintings use colour in this way. Jean looked more to the example of Richard Paul Lohse, whose painting she deeply admired, but his method of working through the spectrum across a square grid did not serve her needs. She wanted to work with the full possibilities that colours offer — their hue, their tone or value, and their intensity — envisaging "a three-dimensional array in which each and every colour has a unique location."

Her text for the "Testing the System" catalogue reads almost like a recipe. Starting with two canvases, each divided into three areas (two rectangles and an open C, related to each other in the ratio 1:2:3), and four fully saturated colours, she set out with just three rules on the disposition of colour: the saturated colours occupying the smallest areas, each colour being present in each canvas, and tonal values being equally distributed. From thereon it was a matter of lightening and darkening colours with white, black or complementaries, so that a colour would begin to lose something of its own identity and gain an affinity with others; thus colours would begin to question and break down geometric divisions, and, at the same time, an overall balance might be achieved.

One cannot escape the sense that this was also her model for life.

Michael Harrison
June 2006

1966: Construction, plywood/PVA

On Working With Jean

This short memoir of Jean Spencer is about our working relationship rather than our close personal friendship, because that is the emphasis that Jean herself would have wanted. For her, the project that was Systematic Constructive Art came first, and with that went a series of extraordinary partnerships and collaborations.

Jean and I first met in 1982 in her kitchen in Putney, South-West London. I was a sociologist intent on studying how artists work and had just started a research project with her partner, Malcolm Hughes. This project involved exchanging resources and hinged on the importance for Constructivist artists of natural scientific knowledge. I could offer Malcolm access to a network of sociologists of scientific knowledge (my colleagues at York University); in return, he had agreed to introduce me to twenty-three working British Constructivist artists, one of whom was Jean. On that occasion in 1982 when Jean and I first met, she came in, said hello and started to prepare a meal. As I carried on demonstrating to Malcolm how an ethnomethodologist would approach an account of social life (!), Jean began tentatively to chip in, gradually contributed more and more (cooking all the while), and, by the end of the demonstration, she and I had done the analysis between us. This impressive feat of making friends by seizing hold of a new subject, grasping it accurately and then enthusiastically helping to apply it was typical of the woman I would soon know well and with whom I was to remain close until her death in 1998.

The research project proceeded apace and all twenty-three artists were interviewed on separate occasions. During each interview, time was set aside for the artist to raise topics which he or she considered important and which had not been covered so far. The most commonly raised topic was art and politics, and the second was, more specifically, the relationship of Constructivist art practice to that of feminism (this was the late 1980s and feminist art practice had a high profile in British art institutions). The art and politics theme is an intriguing one, for each of the twenty-three artists saw their art as having a different relationship to politics, and this has yet to be formally written up and published. The art and feminism theme was followed up. At Jean's suggestion, eight of us (the seven Constructivist artists who were women plus myself) decided to hold regular meetings to explore the topic further. We wanted to ask, in what ways was Constructivist art already feminist and how could current Constructivist art practice address feminist issues? Jean chose our name, "Countervail", and provided much of the momentum — discipline, seniority, ideas, administration and sheer quality artwork — that stimulated us to meet and work regularly together for several years. "Countervail" exhibited, first at Sheffield's Mappin Art Gallery and then for three years at York University, where I taught and where the exhibition and the artists themselves became incorporated into the Sociology postgraduate teaching programme.[1]

In this way Jean laid the foundations for me of a methodological upheaval, which I shall now explain in a little more detail. In the 1980s, empirical sociologists still distanced themselves from their research subjects. They reported back on their "findings" as objectively as possible to fellow researchers via articles in books and learned journals. Many still do. But feminism, as shown in my relationship to the "Countervail" artists, ran counter to that ideology. We worked together. I worked with the Constructivist artists who were women, rather than on them. As well as writing introductions to the shows, Jean encouraged me to produce artworks, which I eventually did. It was immensely exciting to be accepted by the women on their own terms. (The empirical sociologists would have termed this "going native".) And because the "Countervail" work was predominantly visual, I began to focus increasingly on the relationship between verbal sociology and the visual culture of Constructivist art — and indeed of the world outside where, it is said, we in the West now see more images in a day than the Victorians saw in a lifetime. With Jean's encouragement and background support, I published a book in 1995 — "Sociology and Visual Representation" — which saw the start of a whole new social science research area known as visual studies or visual culture. In addition, because the "Countervail" exhibitions tied in with my teaching postgraduates on a course about what it was like to do sociological research, the subjects (the artists), their products, the students, the teaching, the feminism, the questions of methodology and the actual process of doing research came together and almost merged. And Jean was the lynchpin for all this. Heady days.

In short, what Jean did for me was to blur the distinction between artist and social scientist. She did this by bringing feminist theory and practice to bear on that distinction. Quite simply, in her working relationship with me and my sociological project, she demonstrated what feminism was all about. Shortly after her death in 1998, sociology would become, for many scholars, including feminist scholars, an element of the wider field of cultural studies. Visual art would become part of that field too, in the form of critical art theory and practice. But together we had created a piece of cultural studies, combining cultural objects and cultural criticism, in advance of the general trend.

Elizabeth Chaplin.
January 2006

[1]*The "Countervail Collective" comprised Jean Spencer, Judith Dean, Susan Tebby, Nicole Charlett, Tam Giles, Elizabeth Chaplin, Natalie Dower and Jane Wilbraham.*

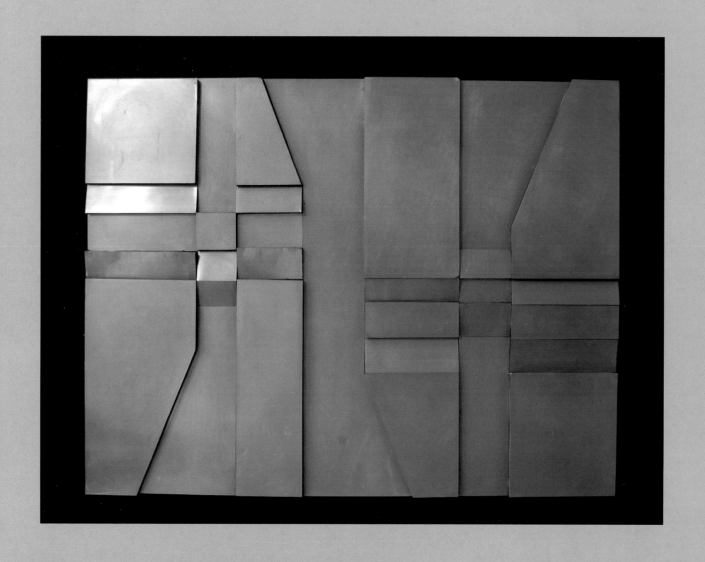

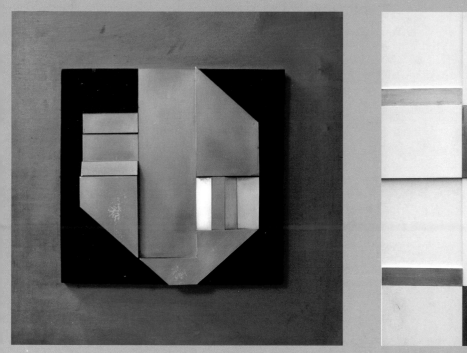

13

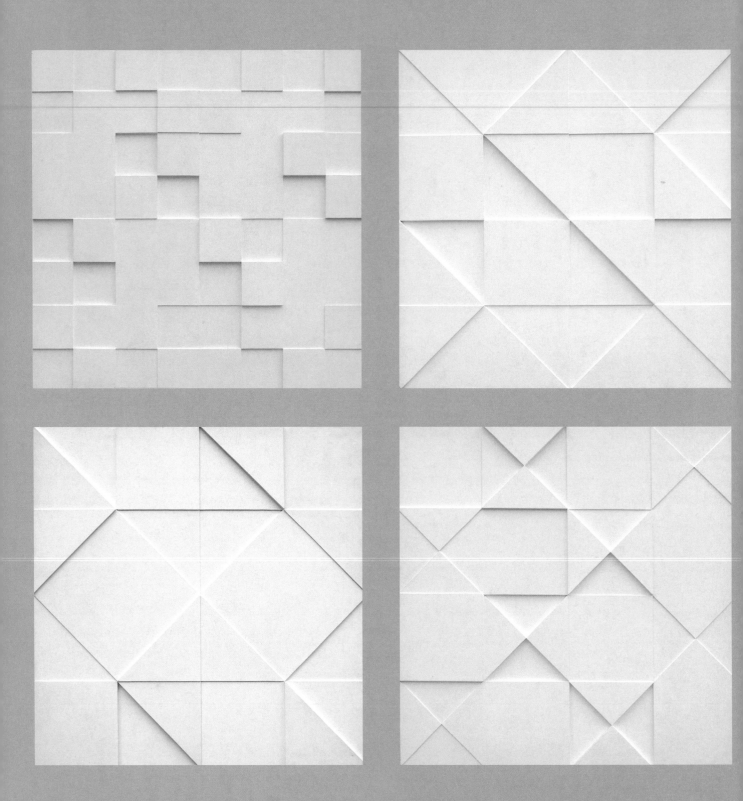

14

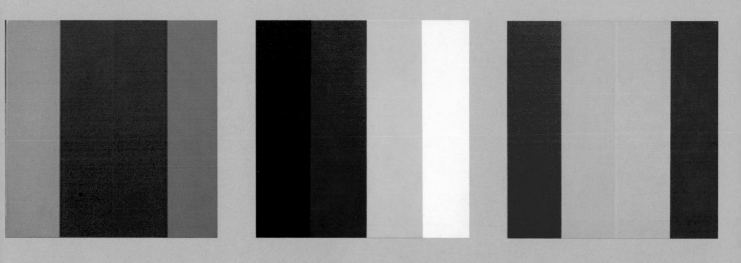

Page	Date	Title	Medium	Dimensions	Source
13 top	1965	Construction	Aluminium on fibre-board on wood, mounted on painted wood	765mm x 1010mm 975mm x 1220mm	Private Collection
13 bottom left	1965	Construction	Aluminium on fibre-board on wood, mounted on painted wood	260mm x 270mm 420mm x 418mm	Private Collection
13 bottom right	1969	Relief	White/Aluminium on wood	760mm x 760mm	Family Collection
14	1976	Four-part Relief, (upper left possibly part of a different series)	Wood on PVA	each 610mm x 610mm	Family Collection
15 top	1989	Three-Part Painting	Oil on linen	3 panels each 500mm x 500mm	Family Collection
15 bottom	1981	Two-by-Three Painting	Oil on linen	2 panels each 1000mm x 1135mm	Family Collection
16 top left and right	1992	Double Square Painting (1)	Oil on linen	350mm x 350mm	Churchill College, Cambridge
16 bottom left and right	1992	Double Square painting (2)	Oil on linen	350mm x 350mm	Churchill College, Cambridge
17 top	1992	BaGaGe project	Case formed from corrugated card, contains: texts, notes, drawings, diagrams, four drawings in pastel	Approx 300mm x 420mm	Location unknown
17 bottom	1994	Countervail 4 Project	Stained glass and rigid box material (possibly plywood), electric light source	4 boxes each approx 400mm x 300mm	Exhibited King's Manor, York believed destroyed
18 top	1993	Untitled, one of a set of two	Hand-made pastel on paper	700mm x 500mm	Collection Mondriaanhuis, Netherlands
18 bottom	1993	Untitled, one of a set of two	Hand-made pastel on paper	700mm x 500mm	Family Collection
19	1996	Studies for Tate paintings (untitled)	Gouache on paper	paper size 680mm x 1060mm image size 530mm x 860mm	Family Collection
20	1996	Series of slides taken by artist.	35mm colour slides		Family Archive

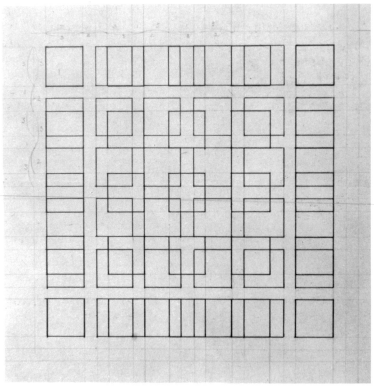

1972: Grid 3.13.1, 3.2.3.2, Drawing on paper

The Systems Group: 1969–1976

Towards the end of 1969 a number of English artists came together in an exhibition in Helsinki entitled *Systeemi-Systems: an Exhibition of Syntactic Art from Britain.* The show's organiser, Jeffrey Steele (b. 1931), had been invited to exhibit in Finland through a friend of his Finnish wife. He assembled a group of nine artists – most known to each other through various teaching contacts – for whom the primary interest was the internal logic of the abstract art work. The terms "system" and "syntactic" in the show's title referred to the concept of the painting or relief being constructed from a vocabulary of largely geometric forms in accordance with pre-determined and often mathematically-based structural systems, with the use of colour influenced by systems of colour relationships.

Immediately after this exhibition, Steele and Malcolm Hughes (1920-1997) invited the artists involved to form the Systems Group, with the aim of promoting interest in an essentially rational approach to art. In common with previous art groups in Britain, the Systems Group had no formal membership arrangements, and involvement in its discussions and exhibitions was a matter of individual choice and invitation. In practice, there were seven members who met most frequently and were involved in all or most of the Group's exhibitions: Steele, Hughes, Colin Jones (b. 1943), Peter Lowe (b. 1938), Michael Kidner (b. 1917), Jean Spencer (1942-1998), and Gillian Wise (b. 1938). Others who participated in the Group's activities from time to time included Richard Allen (b. 1933), John Ernest (1922-1994), James Moyes (b. 1937) and David Saunders (b. 1936).

The Group had several connections with members of the Constructionist Group of the 1950s. Lowe and Jones had been students of Kenneth and Mary Martin. Wise had worked with Anthony Hill. Ernest had exhibited with the Constructionists. All saw themselves, and were seen by contemporary commentators, as working within a broad Constructivist tradition of which Victor Pasmore, the Martins and Hill had been the first British post-war exponents. Hill was a particularly important influence, though he declined an invitation to join the Systems Group. His intense interest in the use of underlying mathematical systems or structures was combined with an emphasis on the production of work which was aesthetically satisfying – a point echoed by John Ernest who once said: "I am trying to achieve some of the beauty of a mathematical system in a visual experience"[1].

The Systems Group's first UK exhibition was at the Arnolfini Gallery in Bristol in 1971, followed by an Arts Council show termed simply *Systems*, which opened at the Whitechapel Gallery in London in March 1972 and then toured the country, finishing at the Museum of Modern Art in Oxford in May 1973. In an explanatory discussion with the art historian Stephen Bann, Malcolm Hughes stated that the show's objective was to promote "a modern, classical and non-utopian art based on the idea of order with endless variety"[2]. By the term "modern", Hughes aligned the artists' emphasis on rationality with the intense interest in the 1970s in science and technology. His reference to classicism reflected the Group's concern for systems of compositional proportion, balance and measurement which had characterised the art and architecture of the Greeks. This included the use of arithmetical phenomena such as the Fibonacci number series and the properties of prime numbers in the systems by which the imagery of much of the Group's work was structured. The phrase "non-utopian" distinguished the Group's philosophy from earlier Constructivist idealism, which had claimed that Constructive art could contribute to the development of an ideal society. For Systems Group artists, perception of the work was the object of its existence, and their concern was for its internal logic, not any actual or theoretical social function. In referring to order with endless variety, Hughes was commenting on the fact that self-imposed limitation to rational systems did not result in a limited range of visual outcomes, rather the reverse, as the very diverse range of visual imagery from the Group's members indicated.

In 1973, the Group held an exhibition at the Polytechnic of Central London entitled *Systems II*. During the early 1970s several members also had individual or small group shows at the Lucy Milton Gallery in Notting Hill. For a few years, this gallery provided a unique showcase in London for the work of European and British artists working in the Constructivist tradition. Its closure in 1975 exacerbated the increasing difficulty the Group's members were experiencing in being recognised by the influential British art establishment. An Arts Council exhibition in 1978, *Constructive Context*, was the last major show in the UK in which Systems art was featured until the inclusion of works by Lowe, Ernest, Steele, Wise and Spencer in an exhibition, *Elements of Abstraction,* co-curated by the author at Southampton City Art Gallery in 2005. This situation contrasted with the growing reputation and frequent showing of these artists throughout the seventies, eighties, and nineties in Germany, Switzerland, Holland, Italy and Poland.

The Group itself dissolved early in 1976, largely as a result of political differences. Some wanted it to adopt an overtly Marxist position, attacking the promotion by the art establishment of what they perceived as irrational art which served the purposes of a capitalist society. Others objected to this, arguing, in the words of Peter Lowe, that they were engaged in "apolitical visual research that had nothing to do with art as ideology"[3]. Despite these differences, most of the Group's members remained personal friends, continued to develop their concepts of systematic Constructive art, and often exhibited together. Following the deaths of Malcolm Hughes and Jean Spencer in 1997 and 1998, the surviving former members of the Group who remain the most active in 2006 are Jeffrey Steele, Peter Lowe and Gillian Wise. They continue to produce art which appeals to the eye for its purity of form and harmony of colour and compositional structure, and to the mind for the subtlety of its underlying rational systems.

Dr Alan Fowler

Notes
1. John Ernest, "Some Thoughts on Mathematics", *Structure*, February 1961, pp 49-51
2. Malcolm Hughes, "Notes on the Context of Systems", *Studio International*, May 1972, pp 200-203
3. Peter Lowe, correspondence with the author, March 2005

Jean Spencer: Extracts from Catalogues and Unpublished Writings

1963: Construction, wood

University of Sussex Exhibition 1969, *Catalogue Entry*

These reliefs are not concerned with any form of representation, either of the physical world, or of absolutes of geometry or number. Though involving mathematical procedures, these are employed primarily as a method of investigation; that is, the regulating structure of the relief is in no way dictated by mathematical concepts, rather evolved through a series of discussions which involve mathematical disciplines, but remain fundamentally intuitive.

The work falls into distinct categories: drawings of an intuitive, exploratory nature; diagrams, extended to maquettes, concerned with the rationalisation of the initial statement; and working drawings leading to the final relief.

The initial framework of each relief is the square and its projection into the cube. The central vertical and horizontal axes logically divide the structure into four units, which by the nature of the symmetry of the cube, are interchangeable. A secondary grid is formed through the investigation of the linear construction of the cube. Each unit on its own is essentially a flat, linear structure; the juxtaposition of four sets up two homogeneous, yet at the same time conflicting disciplines, the first, derived from the initial cube format, with obvious spatial implications, the second, a related, but essentially two-dimensional grid, whose relative spatial position at any one time is ambiguous.

Within certain clearly defined limits the units remain at all times interchangeable and the number of valid combinations under even the simplest of systems very great, so that despite a detailed investigation of the symmetrical/spatial/geometrical properties of the units and their relations, the final decision relative to the artefact must be intuitive. Within each series of reliefs the first is concerned with a direct use of the units; subsequently the rigid framework of the units is broken down.

These later reliefs could not exist without the initial discipline.

These works cannot be approached exclusively through either the emotions or the intellect; they represent an area common to both: a rationalised intuition.

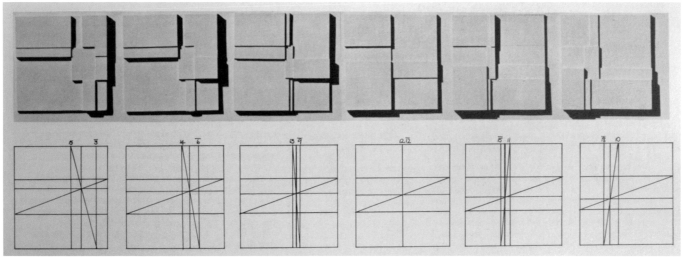

1972: maquette for Relief 1, drawing for Relief 1

"Systems" Exhibition 1972, *Catalogue Statement*

"He was a man capable of disinterested action, of unostentatious generosity, that does not necessarily mean a man of feeling, nor a pleasant man, nor a scrupulous, nor a truthful, nor even a good man. A partial goodness, in which there persisted, perhaps, a trace of the family whom my great-aunt had known, existed probably in him in view of this action before I discovered it, as America or the North Pole existed before Columbus or Peary. Nevertheless, at the moment of my discovery M. Verdurin's nature offered me a new and unimagined aspect; and so I am brought up against the difficulty of presenting a permanent image as well of a character as of societies and passions. For it changes no less than they, and if we seek to portray what is relatively unchanging in it, we see it present, in succession, different aspects (implying that it cannot remain still, but keeps moving) to the disconcerted artist."

Proust, *Remembrance of Things Past*

The expression "System" is intended to convey the total structuring forces present in the work — conceptual, plastic, methodological, material. It is through the interdependence and cross-fertilisation of these forces that the work evolves, rather than by application of pre-existing formulae.

Out of an investigation of informal plastic relationships certain number sequences may emerge which in turn provide more rigorous structuring for the visual counterpart; the evolution of the system depends on this dialogue between abstract numerical form and visual counterpart, and the dialogue itself can eventually be identified as a method, or set of procedures, upon which other forces can feed. In the process, the abstract system inevitably becomes more sophisticated (though I am not primarily concerned with elegance). A painting or relief represents a simultaneous crystallisation of ideas within each sphere.

The abstract systems cannot be applied in any context other than that in which they evolved — either to a different formal element within the same piece (such as a geometrically evolved sequence grafted on to a tone sequence) or to another version of the piece employing the same information, nor can its method necessarily be followed in further investigations. These are not arbitrarily applied rules (as such they would be uneconomic and philosophically pointless): rather they have made themselves evident in the process of working and testify to the triviality of the conceptual system in the wider context of mathematical thinking. Similarly, the physical material employed has little intrinsic value.

Work Since 1975

Since 1975 my work has made use of a set of simple elements and a legislating matrix. Until recently the primary and determining structure derived from the geometry of the square. Colour (tone, hue) and relief were used to denote specific relations (sequence, opposition, exclusion ...) produced through the interaction of the inherent symmetries of the elements and those generated by the matrix. In these works the presence and nature of the matrix can only be extrapolated from the complete series which displays all the permutations of a particular set of elements (*Four Paintings, 1978*).

In current work geometric relations are governed by colour relations, initially ordered in a colour matrix. In these works chromatic complexity supersedes geometric complexity. The system no longer requires all permutations for its complete exposition, but seeks those structures in which all colour elements are present and identified relations are logically and economically organised. Structure, then, is less determined by "natural" forces than produced towards projected ends. Projected ends are identified out of intrinsic qualities.

Jean Spencer
1978

1979: Motovun Relief, paper

"britisch-systematisch", *Statement on Developments: 1990*

The works of mine in this exhibition were made between 1969 and 1989. They have been selected to represent my practice of twenty years. My commentary on this work is retrospective and partial and, inevitably, it tries to make sense, to reveal a pattern, a consistency of purpose. In each of these works is a question about legislation: how material, sensuous objects are ordered, organised, regulated, governed.

1969: "The regulating structure of the relief ... is evolved through a series of discussions which involve mathematical disciplines, but remain fundamentally intuitive."

1972: "The final form of the relief aims at clarity and economy; an explicit statement of the sense (not essence) rather than the entire mechanics of the system."

1974: "In the making of each work, system and object evolve together. In the case of the coloured square studies, the position and colour of each square is dictated by the system, but the system is as it is because of the nature of squares and colours."

1976: "These drawings are part of a series of works using two overlaid grids and a (legislating) matrix. The grids are defined by area as in a chequer-board (presence/absence). The matrix orders the sequence of disjunction and conjunction."

1979: "Structure, then, is less determined by 'natural' forces than produced towards projected ends. Projected ends are identified out of intrinsic qualities."

1986: "The system explores the geometric/chromatic characteristics of '16' (quaternity, complementarity, opposition, orthogonality, diagonality)... A systematic ordering of colours in a two or three-dimensional space is called a colour array; certain markers in the array offer a basis for structuration: the value scale of the spectrum colours; the binary opposition of complementary colours, the so-called primary colours ..."

1989: "A conception of colour as an ordered array, with a potential for structural meaning, has informed my painting since the early 1970s. More recently I have come to the view that although the array exists 'in nature' we can't know it. What we do know are various representations of it. That is the colour array is not an universal 'natural' phenomenon (existing 'out there' or in some innate structuring of the human brain), but a set of culture-specific categories. At present I'm interested in whether such a set constitutes a system."

In 1979 R.P. Lohse spoke of "Systematic construction in art" as a parallel, analogous to the structure of our society ... What is envisaged is a non-hierarchical, transparent social structure. I think we must still aspire to this. Laws, and forms, are at the same time means to and expressions of ends, and we have to accept value as always present. In painting, I formulate this law because I think that its effect will be "good"; the "objectivity" of systems is tempered by the envisaging of valued effects.

Mary Martin wrote (in 1963): "The essence (of the relief) is the parting from and clinging to a SURFACE ... the space which lies between the surface and the highest point of relief becomes a sphere of play, or conflict... representing the desire to break away and the inability to leave."

I hope it is not too fanciful to suggest that colours have desires and that it is the function of laws, or systems, to regulate these. And the spectator, or respondent, has the right (duty?) to ask of a painting, as of a piece of social legislation, "What kind of regulation is imposed on these sensuous subjects? What limit does it place on their being? To what purpose?"

Jean Spencer
London 1989

Jean Spencer at work in the New Hall Studio during her Churchill College residency, 1997

Artists and "Readers", *Artist's Talk at Kettle's Yard*

"Looking, even seeing, doesn't carry a natural burden of 'thinking' despite the commonplace 'I see' when we mean I understand. 'I see' means to grasp in an instant, in a flash, like a light. From the artist's side, inspiration is also said to happen in a moment — a sudden, breath-taking infusion into the mind. In reality, both happen over time and with effort.

These paintings formalise the time of looking (*durée*) by virtue of their serial, almost narrative form. But all paintings unfold in time; they are not so different to music or poetry or film; or the space/time continuum of a building.

What I can tell you about them, as an artist, is in fact very limited, limited to what I know went into their making. After that, we're on equal ground — just looking, making sense. If the paintings are successful, this is as hard for me as it is for you.

So, artists talking about their work is always a risky business, for you as well as for me.

Painters deal with colour in the world - phenomenal colour, colour effect. Pigments mix subtractively; paintings are reflected light. What sense, or meanings, there is in paintings can only be got through the transmission of reflected lights through the human optical system — from retina to cortex to higher cognitive functions — memory, knowledge, reason and feeling.

The painter, then, deals the stuff, material, of pigments and their rules (subtractive mixing), light and its rules (additive mixing), human physiology and its (universal) rules (trichromatic receptors, opponent processing cells), and culture-specific habits (rather than rules) of looking and thinking.

I'm interested in the relation between all these and especially how universal/cultural predispositions to colour structures can be harnessed to the reading of colour in paintings."

Cambridge 1997

Jean Spencer at work in her studio

Curriculum Vitae

1942   Born in Hampshire – Died 1998

Education

1960-63	Bath Academy of Art, Corsham: Certificate in Education (Painting) (Bristol University)
1978-79	University of Sussex: MA (History & Theory of Art)
1963-67	Teaching at Wychwood School, Oxford
1968	Teaching at Loughborough College of Art
1969-88	Teaching, Department of Art, Bulmershe College of Higher Education, Reading
1980-88	Appointed Head of Department, Principal Lecturer
1988	Appointed Tutor to Students and Secretary to the Slade, Slade School of Fine Art, UCL
1995	Appointed Reader in Fine Art, Slade School of Fine Art, UCL.
1968-75	Member of "Systems" group of artists
1977	Member of "arbeitskreis", international workgroup for systematic Constructive art
1976-79	Produced "Working Information", a series of publications of artists' drawings
1981-83	Member Southern Arts Regional Arts Association Art Panel
1983-88	Co-organiser programmes of exhibitions, lectures, discussions and recitals, Exhibiting Space, London
1990-94	Co-founder, "Countervail" group

One-Person Exhibitions

1965	1	Bear Lane Gallery, Oxford (catalogue text: Norbert Lynton, the Bear Lane also commissioned a short film, directed by John Birt, later purchased by the Arts Council of Great Britain)
1969	2	The Arts Centre, University of Sussex, Brighton (catalogue text: artist)
1974	3	Didsbury College of Education, Manchester (catalogue text: artist)
1980	4	Sally East Gallery, London (catalogue text: artist)
1986	5	Gallery Grare, Paris
1994	6	Galerie Vromans, Gebouw Atrium, Amsterdam
	7	"workfortheeyetodo", a small commissioned installation for an artists' book centre Woburn Gallery, Slade School of Fine Art, UCL, London
2006	9	Jean Spencer: A Retrospective Exhibition, The Yarrow Gallery, Oundle School, Oundle (catalogue text: Serota, Harrison, et al)

Selected Group Exhibitions

1964	1	AIA Gallery, London with Kenneth Robinson, Michael Tyzak (catalogue text: Jules Goddard)
1966	2	Midland Group, Nottingham
	3	"Constructions", Axiom Gallery, London
1967	4	"Unit, Series Progression", Arts Council of Great Britain (catalogue text: Hugh Evans
	5	John Moores Liverpool Exhibition (minor prize)
1968	6	Arts Council of Great Britain Collection Touring Exhibition
1969	7	"Systeemi", Amos Anderson Museum, Helsinki (catalogue text: Jeffrey Steele)
1971	8	"Matrix", Arnolfini Gallery, Bristol (catalogue text: artists)
1972	9	"Systems", Whitechapel Art Gallery, London, ACGB tour (catalogue texts: Stephen Bann; artists)
	10	"Systems", Lucy Milton Gallery, London 1973
	11	"Plus Kern", Ghent, with Malcolm Hughes
	12	"Systems II", Polytechnic of Central London (catalogue texts: Philip Steadman; artists)
1975-76	13	"Rational Concepts: English and Dutch Drawing", Kunstcentrum Badhuis, Gorinchem, Holland
	14	"de volle maan 22: English and Netherlandish Rational Concepts", (texts: artists)
1977	15	"Sul Concetto di Serie", Museo di Mirabello, Varese (catalogue texts: AlbertaVecca, Hans Heinz Holz)
1978	16	"Constructive Context", Warehouse Gallery, London (catalogue texts: Stephen Bann; artists)
	17	"Rational Practice", Gardner Arts Centre, University of Sussex, Brighton (catalogue texts: Norbert Lynton; artists)

1978	18	"Prinzip Seriell: der IAFKIG und Freunde", Galerie Circulus, Bonn (catalogue texts: Hans Heinze Holz; artists)
1978-79	19	John Moores Liverpool Exhibition XT
1979	20	The International Collection for the Laski Children, Galeria Zapiecek, Warsaw
1979-80	21	Kunstlerbucher, Galerie Lydia Megert, Bern
1979	22	"Theorie und Praxis der Konstruktiven Kunst Heute", Arbeitskreis Symposium, Schloss Buchberg, Austria (catalogue texts: Stephen Bann, Dieter Bogner)
	23	"Transformacije papira", 7th Motovun Meeting, Motovun, Yugoslavia (catalogue texts: Norbert Lynton; artists)
1980	24	"Modern British Abstracts", Glasgow Art Gallery and Museum
	25	"Arbeitskreis: Motovun 79", Polytechnic of Central London (curated and produced by Jean Spencer; catalogue texts: artist;)
1982	26	"Concepts in Construction: 1910-1980 Independent Curators Incorporated, New York, travelling exhibition (curated and with catalogue text by Irving Sandler)
1982	27	"South Bank Show", South London Art Gallery
1983	28	"Nature, Structure, Construction: Arbeitskreis Lapissa in Lapland", Kemin Taidemuseo, Kemin, Finland (catalogue text: Paul Hefting)
1984	29	"Constructive Tendencies in Europe", Galerie Konstructiv Tendens, Stockholm
	30	"Exhibition 2: Drawings", Exhibiting Space, London
1985	31	"Arbeitskreis; Work in Progress", Kunstation, Kleinsassen, Germany
	32	"Boundaries", Exhibiting Space, London
1986	33	"Kunststrasse Rhon", Kleinsassen, Germany (a major work in sixteen parts, one for each of the sixteen villages in the Hofbieber district; catalogue texts: artists)
	34	"Colour Presentations: paintings by six artists working within a systematic constructive practice", travelling exhibition sponsored by the Welsh Arts Council: Gardner Centre Gallery, University of Sussex; Wrexham Library Arts Centre; Spacex Gallery, Exeter; Swiss Cottage Library, London; Stoke on Trent Museum and Art Gallery (catalogue text: Bernard Harrison)
	35	Paintings by Trevor Clarke, Jean Spencer, G.R.Thomson, "Exhibiting Space", London
1987	36	"Exhibiting Space", Ruskin College, Oxford
	37	"Systematic Constructive Drawings", Wentworth Gallery, University of York (catalogue texts: Elizabeth Chaplin; artists)
1988/9	38	"Null-dimension", Galerie New Space, Fulda, Germany; Kunst International Konstructive Stromungen, Austria
1989	39	"Konkret 9", Kunsthaus Nurnberg, Germany (catalogue texts: Diet Sayler; artists)
	40	"Re-Views: contemporary systematic and constructive arts", Small Mansion Arts Centre, London (catalogue texts: Robin Kinross; artists)
	41	"Arte Systematico y Constructivo", Centro Cultural de la Villa, Madrid
	42	"Arbeitskreis", Muzeu Okregowe, Chelm, Poland; invited participant in 7th Summer School Okuninka, Chelm
	43	"Homage a Henryk Stazewski", Galeria Rekwizytornia, Wroclow, Poland
1989-90	44	"From Prism to Paintbox: Colour Theory and Practice in Modern British Painting" touring exhibition organised by the Oriel Gallery, Mold (catalogue text: Roy Osborne)
1990	45	"Britisch-systematisch", Stiftung fur konstruktive und konkrete Kunst, Zurich (catalogue texts: Stephen Bann; artists)
1992	46	"Countervail", Mappin Art Gallery, Sheffield; Mead Gallery, University of Warwick, Coventry (catalogue texts: artists)
1993	47	"BaGaGe", Galerie de Lawei, Drachten, Holland (catalogue texts: artists)
	48	"Raum Klang Bild", Symposon fur bildende kunst und musik in Gmunden, Austria
	49	"Moving into View", a display of the Arts Council Collection, Royal Festival Hall, London
	50	"Countervail 3", JB Morrell Library Foyer, University of York
1994	51	"BaGaGe", Galerie Vromans, Amsterdam
	52	"Countervail 4", Kings Manor Gallery, York
1996	53	"Farbe Konkrete Kunst", Haus Dacheroden, Erfurt, Germany
	54	"Ten Artists from the British Isles", J.N.J. Gallery, Prague
	55	"Testing the System", Kettle's Yard, Cambridge

Works in Public Collections

Arts Council of Great Britain
Birmingham Museum and Art Gallery
Chelsea School of Art, Library
Churchill College, Cambridge
Leicester Schools Collection
Liverpool City Council
New Hall College, Cambridge
Manchester City Art Gallery
Mead Gallery, Warwick
Mondriaanhuis, Amersfoort, Netherlands
Reading Museum
Southampton City Gallery and Museum
Tate
Various private collections in UK and Europe

Published Texts (excluding catalogue texts)

1977	1	"Survey of British and European Constructed Relief Artists", ed. Donald McNamee; *The Structurist*, Number 17/18, 1977/78 pp 101-117
1985	2	"Notes towards a working definition of boundaries, Exhibiting Space, 1985 Autumn Programme Conspectus, Exhibiting Space, London pp 97-99
1996	3	Colloquium paper for "Farbe Konkrete Kunst": "Towards a theory of constructive Colour", Haus Dacheroden, Erfurt, 1996

Unpublished Conference Papers

1987	1	Report on the Kleinsassen Project: 16 Part Painting, Exhibiting Space, London
1989	2	Exhibiting Space, London 1984-89: "Theory, practice, discourse", Co-audio-visual presentation; "Arbeitskreis, concept and aims": Symposium of Systematic and Constructive Art, Centro Cultual de la Villa, Madrid
1990	3	Paper on colour and painting, "Symposium: Zehn Jahre konkrete Nurnberg", Nurnberg, Germany

Archives of Jean Spencer Documents

Chelsea College of Art and Design, The London Institute
Hyman Kreitman Research Centre, Tate Britain
Family Archive, Reading, contact Marian Waters, d.g.waters@btopenworld.com